ACCA
Financial Management (FM)

First edition 2007, Thirteenth edition January 2019

ISBN 9781 5097 2396 6

e ISBN 9781 5097 2423 9

British Library Cataloguing-in-Publication Data

A catalogue record for this book is available from the British Library

Published by

BPP Learning Media Ltd
BPP House, Aldine Place
142–144 Uxbridge Road
London W12 8AA

www.bpp.com/learningmedia

Printed in the United Kingdom

Welcome to BPP's Learning Media's, ACCA **Passcards for Financial Management (FM)**.

- They **focus on your exam** and **save you time**.

- They incorporate **diagrams** to kick start your memory.

- They follow the overall **structure** of the BPP Learning Media's Study Texts, but BPP Learning Media's ACCA **Passcards** are not just a condensed book. Each card has been separately designed for clear presentation. Topics are self contained and can be grasped visually.

- ACCA **Passcards** are still **just the right size** for pockets, briefcases and bags.

Run through the **Passcards** as often as you can during your final revision period. The day before the exam, try to go through the **Passcards** again! You will then be well on your way to passing your exams.

Good luck!

For reference to the Bibliography of the Financial Management Passcards please go to learningmedia.bpp.com and visit the "Student" section.

Contents

1: Financial management and financial objectives

Topic List

Financial management

Objectives

Stakeholders

Measuring achievement of objectives

Encouraging achievement of objectives

Not-for-profit organisations

This chapter provides a definition of financial management and objectives and provides the background for your study of this subject.

You must be able to choose appropriate measures and indicators of an organisation's situation and discuss whether objectives have been achieved.

Financial accounting →
- Provides **externally** used information
- **Historic** picture of **past** operations

Management accounting →
- Provides **internally** used information
- Used to aid management to **record, plan** and **control** activities and help the **decision-making** process

Financial management →
- **Financial planning** – making sure funds available
- **Financial control** – objectives being met and assets being used efficiently

Financial management decisions →
- **Financing**, taking more credit, profit retention, issuing shares
- **Dividends**
- **Investing**, to maximise company's value

Strategy is a course of action to achieve an objective. **Corporate strategy** is concerned with the overall purpose and scope of the organisation.

Corporate objectives are relevant for the organisation as a whole, relating to key factors for business success.

Financial objectives	**Non-financial objectives**
■ Shareholder wealth maximisation ■ Profit maximisation ■ Earnings per share growth	■ Welfare of employees ■ Welfare of management, perks, benefits ■ Welfare of society, eg green policies ■ Provision of certain level of service ■ Responsibilities towards customers/suppliers

Stakeholders

Are groups whose interests are directly affected by activities of the organisation.

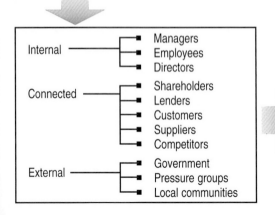

Internal
- Managers
- Employees
- Directors

Connected
- Shareholders
- Lenders
- Customers
- Suppliers
- Competitors

External
- Government
- Pressure groups
- Local communities

Stakeholder objectives

- **Ordinary shareholders** want to maximise their wealth.

- **Suppliers** want to be paid full amount at due date and to continue trading relationship.

- **Banks** want to receive interest and minimise default risk.

- **Employees** want to maximise rewards and ensure employment continuity.

- **Managers** want to maximise their own rewards.

- **Government** wants sustained economic growth and high levels of employment.

Returns to shareholders

Returns to shareholders
- Dividends
- Capital gains from increases in market value

Profitability

Return on capital employed = **Profit margin** × **Asset turnover**
(ROCE)

$$\frac{PBIT}{Capital\ employed} = \frac{PBIT}{Sales\ revenue} \times \frac{Sales\ revenue}{Capital\ employed}$$

Return on equity = $\dfrac{Profit\ available\ to\ ordinary\ shareholders}{Shareholders'\ equity}$

PBIT = profit before interest and tax

Dividend yield

$$\frac{\text{Dividend per share}}{\text{Ex-div market price per share}} \times 100\%$$

Dividend cover

$$\frac{\text{Profit available to ordinary shareholders}}{\text{Actual dividend}}$$

Price earnings ratio

$$\frac{\text{Market price of share}}{\text{EPS}}$$

P/E ratio reflects market's appraisal of share's future prospects.

Earnings per share (EPS)

$$\frac{\text{Profit available to ordinary shareholders}}{\text{Weighted average number of ordinary shares}}$$

Agency relationship

Managers act as agents for the shareholders using delegated powers to run the company in shareholders' best interests.

Encouraging the achievement of stakeholder objectives

Regulatory requirements

Managerial reward schemes

- Performance-related pay
- Rewarding managers with shares
- Share option schemes

Corporate governance

- The system by which organisations are directed and controlled.
- Involves risk management, internal controls, accountability to stakeholders, conducting business in an ethical and effective way.

Stock exchange listing regulations

Rules and regulations to ensure the stock market operates fairly and efficiently.

Not-for-profit organisation

Is an organisation whose attainment of its prime goal is not assessed by economic measures.

Value for money

Is getting the best possible combination of services from the least resources.

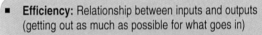

- **Efficiency:** Relationship between inputs and outputs (getting out as much as possible for what goes in)
- **Effectiveness:** Relationship between outputs and objectives (getting done what was supposed to be done)
- **Economy:** Obtaining the right quality and quantity of inputs at lowest cost (being frugal)

Problems of measuring VFM

- Multiple objectives
- Meaningful measurement of outputs
- Subjective assessment

2–3: Financial management environment

Businesses must operate in an economy in which the government is trying to achieve its objectives. The economic environment will impact on a business's activities and future plans.

Financing of a business takes place through financial markets and institutions.

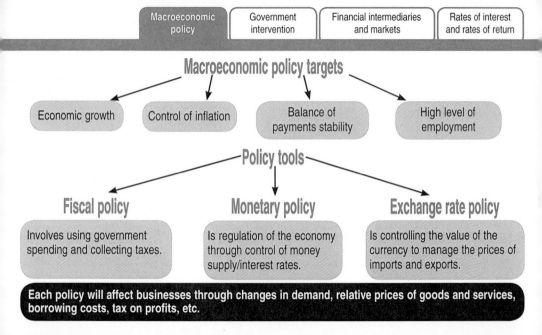

Macroeconomic policy targets

- Economic growth
- Control of inflation
- Balance of payments stability
- High level of employment

Policy tools

Fiscal policy

Involves using government spending and collecting taxes.

Monetary policy

Is regulation of the economy through control of money supply/interest rates.

Exchange rate policy

Is controlling the value of the currency to manage the prices of imports and exports.

Each policy will affect businesses through changes in demand, relative prices of goods and services, borrowing costs, tax on profits, etc.

Regulation

Is any form of state intervention with the operation of the free market.

Competition policy

- To reduce a company's domination of a market
- Controls on prices or profits
- Investigation of mergers
- Investigation of restrictive practices

Government assistance for business

- **Official aid schemes** eg grants for depressed areas
- Severely restricted by EU policies to prevent distortion of free market competition

Green policies

- **Polluter pays** principle eg levy a tax
- **Subsidies** to reduce pollution
- **Legislation** eg waste disposal

Financial intermediaries

Bring together lenders and borrowers of finance.

Examples

- Commercial banks
- Finance houses
- Mutual societies
- Institutional investors

Functions

- Means of lending/investing
- Source of borrowing
- Package amounts lent by savers
- Pool risk
- Provide maturity transformation

Money markets

Are operated by banks/financial institutions and provide means of trading, lending and borrowing in the **short-term**. Markets include primary, Interbank, Eurocurrency and certificate of deposit.

Capital markets

Are markets for trading in **long-term** financial instruments, equities and bonds. They enable organisations to raise new finance and investors to realise investments. Principal UK markets are the Stock Exchange and Alternative Investment Market.

Euromarkets

Are international markets for larger companies to raise finance in a **foreign currency**. (Not necessarily the euro or Europe.)

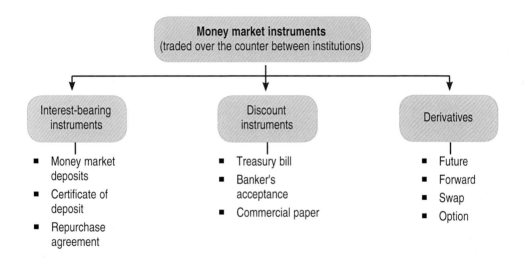

Factors affecting interest rates

Various interest rates are available; they depend on risk, duration, size of loan, likely capital gain.

General factors affecting all rates

- Need for a real return
- Inflation/expectations
- Liquidity preference
- Balance of payments policy
- Monetary policy
- Foreign interest rates

The risk-return trade-off

Investors in riskier assets expect to be compensated for the risk.

Risk ↓

- Government bonds
- Company loan notes
- Preference shares
- Ordinary shares

4: Working capital

Topic List

Working capital

Liquidity ratios

Working capital management is a crucial part of the syllabus and essential for a successful business.

The ratios covered in this chapter are essential to learn.

Working capital = current assets – current liabilities

Working capital management

Minimise risk of insolvency   Maximise return on assets

Cash operating cycle

Is the period of time between the **outflow** of cash to pay for raw materials and the **inflow** of cash from customers.

The average time raw materials remain in inventory	X
Less: the period of credit taken from suppliers	X
Plus: the time taken to produce the goods	X
Plus: the time taken by customers to pay for the goods	X
	X

The longer the cycle, the more money is tied up.

The **optimal length** of the cycle depends on the industry.

Liquidity ratios

Help to indicate whether a company is **over-capitalised**, with excessive working capital, or if a business is likely to **fail**.

$$\text{Current ratio} = \frac{\text{Current assets}}{\text{Current liabilities}}$$

$$\text{Acid test/quick ratio} = \frac{\text{Current assets (excluding inventory)}}{\text{Current liabilities}}$$

Receivables payment period

$$= \frac{\text{Trade receivables}}{\text{Credit sales}} \times 365 \text{ days}$$

$$\text{Payables' payment period} = \frac{\text{Trade payables}}{\text{Purchases}} \times 365 \text{ days}$$

Inventory days

$$= \frac{\text{Average inventory}}{\text{Cost of sales}} \times 365 \text{ days}$$

$$\text{Inventory turnover} = \frac{\text{Cost of sales}}{\text{Average inventory}}$$

Sales revenue/net working capital can be used to forecast the level of working capital needed for a projected level of sales.

Overtrading

Is when a business is trying to support too large a volume of trade with the capital resources at its disposal.

Symptoms	Solutions
■ ↑↑ Revenue	■ Finance from share issues/retained profits
■ ↑↑ Current assets	■ Better inventory/receivables control
■ ↑↑ Non-current assets	■ Postpone expansion plans
■ Asset increases financed by trade payables/bank overdraft	■ Maintain/increase proportion of long-term finance
■ Little/no ↑ in proprietors' capital	
■ ↓ Current/quick ratios	
■ Liquidity deficit	

Low liquidity ratios can provide indications of impending bankruptcy.

5: Managing working capital

Topic List

Managing inventories

Managing accounts receivable

Managing accounts payable

The management of inventories, accounts receivable and accounts payable are key aspects of working capital control. Questions may be set on the financial effect of changing policies and longer questions will probably require a discussion as well as a calculation.

Inventory costs

Holding costs
- Cost of capital
- Warehouse/handling costs
- Deterioration/obsolescence
- Insurance
- Pilferage

Procuring costs
- Ordering costs
- Delivery costs

Shortage costs
- Contribution from lost sales
- Emergency inventory
- Stock-out costs

Re-order level = maximum usage × maximum lead time

Purchase cost

Buffer safety inventory = re-order level − (average usage × average lead time)

Average inventory = buffer safety inventory + $\dfrac{\text{re-order amount}}{2}$

Economic order quantity (EOQ)

Is the optimal ordering quantity for an item of inventory which will minimise costs.

$$EOQ = \sqrt{\frac{2C_O D}{C_H}} \quad \text{(Given in exam)}$$

D = Usage in units (demand)
C_O = Cost of placing one order
C_H = Holding cost
Q = Reorder quantity

Bulk discounts

Total cost will be minimised:

- At pre-discount EOQ level, so that discount not worthwhile; or
- At minimum order size necessary to earn discount

Calculate total inventory cost:

Purchasing costs + Holding costs + Ordering costs

Finally, select the order quantity that minimises total inventory cost.

Just-in-time (JIT)

Describes a policy of obtaining goods from suppliers at the latest possible time, avoiding the need to carry materials/component inventory.

Benefits of JIT	
↓ Inventory holding costs	↓ Labour/scrap/warranty costs
↓ Manufacturing lead times	↓ Material purchase costs (discounts)
↑ Labour productivity	↓ Number of transactions

Cost of offering credit = Value of interest charged on an overdraft to fund the period of credit

or

Interest lost on cash not received and deposited in the bank

Managing receivables involves:

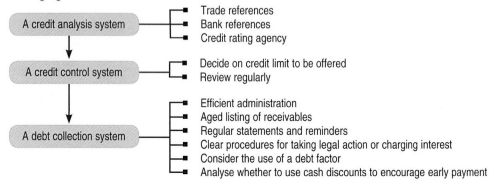

A credit analysis system
- Trade references
- Bank references
- Credit rating agency

A credit control system
- Decide on credit limit to be offered
- Review regularly

A debt collection system
- Efficient administration
- Aged listing of receivables
- Regular statements and reminders
- Clear procedures for taking legal action or charging interest
- Consider the use of a debt factor
- Analyse whether to use cash discounts to encourage early payment

The benefits of action to collect debts must be greater than the costs incurred.

Discounts for early settlement

Calculate:

- Profits forgone by offering discount
- Interest charge changes because customer paid at different times and sales change

Invoice discounting

Similar to factoring, this is when a company sells specific trade debts to another company, at a discount. Invoice discounting helps to improve cash flow at times of temporary cash shortage.

Factoring

Is debt collection by factor company which advances proportion of money due.

Advantages	Disdvantages
☑ Saving in staff time/ admin costs	☒ Can be expensive
☑ New source of finance to help liquidity	☒ Loss of direct customer contact and goodwill
☑ Frees up management time	
☑ Supports a business when sales are rising	

Problems with foreign trade

- Delays due to paperwork
- Transport problems
- Bad debt risks

Larger inventories and accounts receivable

Methods of control

- **Letters of credit**. The customer's bank guarantees it will pay the invoice after delivery of the goods.
- **Bills of exchange**. An IOU signed by the customer, can be sold.
- **Export factoring**
- **Countertrade**. A form of barter with goods exchanged for other goods.
- **Export credit insurance**

Management of trade payables

→ Obtaining satisfactory credit terms

→ Extending credit if cash short

→ Maintain good relations

Foreign accounts payable

Are subject to **exchange rate risk**. Depreciation of a domestic currency will make the cost of supplies more expensive.

Cost of lost cash discounts

$$\left[\left(\frac{100}{100 - d} \right)^{365/t} \right] - 1$$

where d is percentage discount
t is reduction in payment period in days necessary to obtain early discount

6: Working capital finance

The management of cash is the final part of working capital management.

The cash needs of an organisation can be determined using a cash flow forecast and this will allow a business to plan how to deal with expected cash flow surpluses or shortages.

Cash flow forecast

- A detailed forecast of cash inflows and outflows incorporating revenue and capital items
- Clearly laid out with references to workings
- Depreciation is **not** a cash item

Cash forecast

	Jan	Feb	March
Cash receipts	X	X	X
Sales receipts (W1)		X	
Share issue		X	
	X	X	X
Cash payments			
Purchases (W2)	X	X	X
Dividends	X		
Taxes	X		
Purchase of non-current assets		X	
Wages	X	X	X
	X	X	X
Net surplus/deficit	(X)	X	X
Opening cash balance	X	X	X
Closing cash balance	(X)	X	X

Reasons for holding cash

- **Transactions motive** to meet regular commitments

- **Precautionary motive** to maintain a buffer for unforeseen contingencies

- **Speculative motive** to make money from a rise in interest rates

Easing cash flow problems

- Postponing capital expenditure
- Accelerating cash inflows
- Selling non-essential assets
- Longer credit
- Rescheduling loan repayments
- Deferring corporation tax
- Reducing dividend payments

- Losses
- Asset replacement
- Growth support
- Seasonal business
- One-off expenditure

Cash flow problems

Treasury management

Treasury departments are set up to manage cash funds and currency efficiently, and make the best use of corporate finance markets.

The main advantages of centralised treasury management are avoiding a mix of surpluses and overdrafts, and being able to obtain favourable rates on bulk borrowing/investment.

Centralised treasury management

- Improve exchange risk management
- Employ experts
- Smaller precautionary balances required
- Focus on profit centre

Decentralised treasury management

- Finance matches local assets
- Greater autonomy for subsidiaries
- More responsive to operating units
- No opportunities for large sum speculation

Baumol model

Seeks to minimise cash holding costs by calculating optimal amount of new funds to raise.

Miller-Orr model —

→ When cash balance reaches upper limit, firms buys securities to return cash balance to return point (normal level)

→ When cash balance reaches lower limit sell securities to return to return point

Return point = lower limit + ($1/3 \times$ spread)

$$Q = \sqrt{\frac{2CS}{i}}$$

where   S   is the amount of cash used in period

C   is the fixed cost of obtaining new funds

i   is the interest cost of holding cash

Q   is the total amount to be raised to provide for S

May be difficult to predict amounts required and no buffer cash is allowed for.

$$\text{Spread} = 3\left(\frac{3}{4} \times \left(\frac{\text{transaction cost} \times \text{cash flow variance}}{\text{interest rate}} \right) \right)^{1/3}$$

1 Set lower limit for cash balance

2 Estimate variance of cash flow

3 Ascertain interest rate and transaction cost

4 Compute upper limit and return point

6: Working capital finance

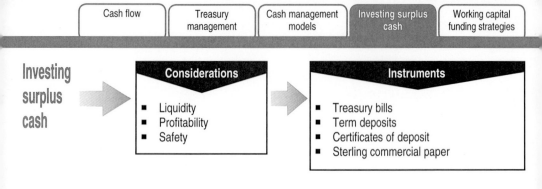

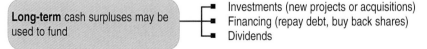

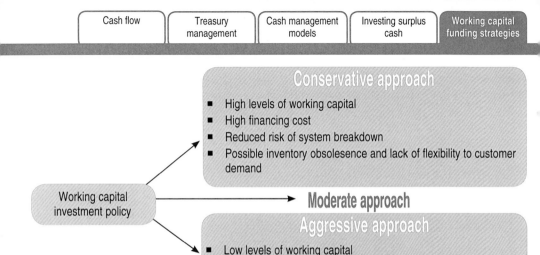

Conservative approach

- High levels of working capital
- High financing cost
- Reduced risk of system breakdown
- Possible inventory obsolesence and lack of flexibility to customer demand

Working capital investment policy

Moderate approach

Aggressive approach

- Low levels of working capital
- Aim to increase profitability by reducing financing cost
- Increased risk of system breakdown and loss of goodwill
- Easier with modern manufacturing techniques

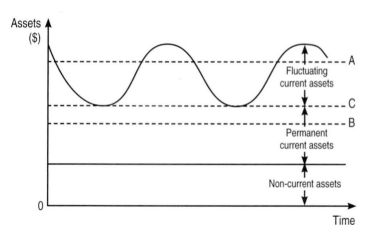

In A (conservative) all permanent and some fluctuating current assets financed out of long-term sources; may be surplus cash for investment.

In B (aggressive) all fluctuating and some permanent current assets financed out of short-term sources, possible liquidity problems.

In C long-term sources finance permanent assets, short-term sources finance fluctuating assets.

Assets above the dotted line are financed by short-term funding while assets below the dotted line are financed by long-term funding.

7: Investment decisions

Topic List

Investment

Payback

Return on capital employed

The investment decision is a major topic in FM and this chapter introduces the basic techniques.

As well as carrying out payback and ROCE calculations, you will also be expected to know their drawbacks.

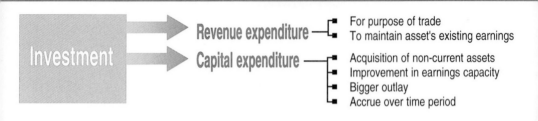

Investment

Revenue expenditure
- For purpose of trade
- To maintain asset's existing earnings

Capital expenditure
- Acquisition of non-current assets
- Improvement in earnings capacity
- Bigger outlay
- Accrue over time period

The investment decision-making process

1 Origination of proposals

2 Project screening

3 Analysis and acceptance

4 Monitoring and review

Relevant cash flows

- Future
- Incremental
- Cash
- No: central overheads, sunk costs, depreciation

Payback

Is the time taken for the cash inflows from a capital investment project to equal the cash outflows, usually expressed in years.

It is used as a minimum target/first screening method.

Example

$'000	P	Q
Investment	60	60
Yr 1 profits	20	50
Yr 2 profits	30	20
Yr 3 profits	50	5

Q pays back first, but ultimately P's profits are higher on the same amount of investment.

Advantages

- ☑ Simple to calculate and understand
- ☑ Concentrates on short-term, less risky flows
- ☑ Can identify quick cash generators

Disadvantages

- ☒ Ignores timing of flows after payback period
- ☒ Ignores total project return
- ☒ Ignores time value of money
- ☒ Arbitrary choice of cut-off

7: Investment decisions

Return on capital employed

- Also known as accounting rate of return or return on investment.

- Can be used to rank projects taking place over a number of years (using average profits and investment).

- Can also rank mutually exclusive projects.

Method of calculation

$$\frac{\text{Estimated average profits}}{\text{Estimated average investment}} \times 100\%$$

Where average investment = $\dfrac{\text{Initial outlay} + \text{scrap value}}{2}$

Profit is **after** depreciation but before interest and tax

Advantages
☑ Quick and simple calculation
☑ Easy to understand % return
☑ Looks at entire project life

Disadvantages
☒ Takes no account of timing
☒ Based on accounting profits, not cash flows
☒ Relative, not absolute, measure
☒ Ignores time value of money
☒ Takes no account of project length

Topic List

Discounted cash flow

NPV

IRR

This is an absolutely critical chapter, as questions requiring the use of NPV and IRR will come up frequently in the exam.

Discounted cash flow analysis applies discounting arithmetic to the costs and benefits of an investment project, reducing value of future cash flows to present value equivalent.

Conventions of DCF analysis

- Cash flows incurred at beginning of project occur in year 0
- Cash flows occurring during time period assumed to occur at period-end
- Cash flows occurring at beginning of period assumed to occur at end of previous period

PV of cash flows in perpetuity

$ cashflow × 1/r

r is cost of capital

Discounting

$$\text{Present value of 1} = \frac{1}{(1+r)^n}$$

Annuity

$$\text{Present value of annuity of 1} = \frac{1-(1+r)^{-n}}{r}$$

r = Discount rate
n = number of periods

Net Present Value (NPV)

Is the value obtained by discounting all cash flows of project by target rate of return/cost of capital. If NPV is positive, the project will be accepted, if negative it will be rejected.

Features of NPV
■ Uses all cash flows related to project
■ Allows timing of cash flows
■ Can be calculated using generally accepted method

Rules of NPV calculations

Include
☑ Effect of tax allowances
☑ After-tax incremental cash flows
☑ Working capital requirements
☑ Opportunity costs

Exclude
☒ Depreciation
☒ Dividend/interest payments
☒ Sunk costs
☒ Allocated costs and overheads

8: Investment appraisal using DCF methods

The IRR (Internal Rate of Return) method calculates the rate of return at which the NPV is zero.

1. Calculate net present value using rate for cost of capital which

   a. Is whole number

   b. May give NPV close to zero

2. Calculate second NPV using a different rate

   a. If first NPV is positive, use second rate greater than first rate

   b. If first NPV is negative, use second rate less than first rate

3. Use two NPV values to calculate IRR

Formula to learn

$$IRR = a + \left(\left(\frac{NPV_a}{NPV_a - NPV_b} \right)(b-a) \right)\%$$

Where

a   Is lower of two rates of return used

b   Is higher of two rates of return used

NPV_a Is NPV obtained using rate a

NPV_b Is NPV obtained using rate b

Advantages of DCF methods

- Take into account time value of money
- Take account of all project's cash flows
- Allow for timing of cash flows
- Universally accepted methods

NPV

- Simpler to calculate
- Better for ranking mutually exclusive projects
- Easy to incorporate different discount rates

NPV and IRR comparison

For conventional cash flows both methods give the same decision.

IRR

- More easily understood
- Can be confused with ROCE
- Ignores relative size of investments
- May be several IRRs if cash flows not conventional

9: Allowing for inflation and taxation

Topic List

Inflation

Taxation

NPV layout

Tax complications are likely to be introduced frequently into NPV calculations. As well as bringing inflation and tax into calculations, in longer questions you could be asked to explain the difference between real and nominal rates of return.

Nominal rate of return measures return in terms of the (falling in value) currency.

Real rate of return measures return in constant price level terms.

Formula (given in exam)

$$(1 + \text{nominal rate}) = (1 + \text{real rate}) \times (1 + \text{inflation rate})$$
$$(1 + i) = (1 + r) \times (1 + h)$$

Real rate or nominal rate?

If cash flows in terms of **actual dollars** received/paid in **various future dates,** use the **nominal rate**

If cash flows in terms of **value of dollar at time 0** (constant price levels) use the **real rate**

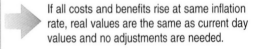
If all costs and benefits rise at same inflation rate, real values are the same as current day values and no adjustments are needed.

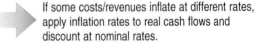
If some costs/revenues inflate at different rates, apply inflation rates to real cash flows and discount at nominal rates.

For DCF calculations, use end of year money values.

Working capital

- Increases in working capital reduce the net cash flow of period
- Relevant cash flows are the incremental cash flows from one year's requirement to next
- Assumed to be recovered at end of project outflows = inflows

Taxation

Follow the instructions given in the question re timing and rates.

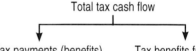

Total tax cash flow

Tax payments (benefits) on operating profit (losses)

Tax benefits from tax allowable depreciation

1 Calculate amount of capital allowance claimed in each year.

2 Don't forget balancing adjustment in year of sale.

3 Calculate tax saved.

	Year 0	Year 1	Year 2	Year 3	Year 4	
Sales receipts		X	X	X		
Costs	___	(X)	(X)	(X)	___	
Sales less Costs		X	X	X		
Taxation on profits		(X)	(X)	(X)	(X)	
Capital expenditure	(X)					
Scrap value				X		
Working capital	(X)			X		
Tax benefit of tax depreciation	___	X	X	X	X	
	(X)	X	X	X	(X)	
Discount factors @ post-tax cost of capital	X	X	X	X	X	NPV is the sum
Present value	(X)	X	X	X	(X)	of present values

10: Project appraisal and risk

Another complication that can be introduced into DCF calculations is uncertainty. You may be asked in the exam to carry out sensitivity analysis on a number of variables or use probabilities when calculating NPV.

The probabilities of a project's outcomes are:

Predictable and quantifiable

Not predictable and not quantifiable

RISK

UNCERTAINTY

- Expected values
- Risk adjusted discount factor
- Certainty equivalents

- Adjusted payback
- Sensitivity analysis
- Simulation

Sensitivity analysis

Assesses how responsive a project's NPV is to changes in the variables used to calculate the NPV.

Variables

- Selling price
- Sales volume
- Cost of capital
- Initial cost
- Operating costs
- Benefits

Weaknesses

- ☒ Only considers one variable at a time
- ☒ Changes in variables often interdependent
- ☒ Takes no account of probabilities
- ☒ Critical factors possibly not controllable
- ☒ Doesn't provide decision rule

$$\text{Sensitivity} = \frac{\text{NPV}}{\text{PV of variance}}$$

Probability analysis

1. Calculate expected value of NPV

2. Measure risk by one of following methods:
   - Calculate worst possible outcome and its probability
   - Calculate probability that project fails to achieve positive NPV

Which project should be selected?

If projects are mutually exclusive and carry different levels of risk, with the less risky project having a lower expected NPV, which project is selected will depend on how risk-averse management are.

Problems with expected values
☒ Investment may be one-off, and expected value not possible outcome
☒ Assigning probabilities may be subjective
☒ Expected values do not indicate range of outcomes

11: Specific investment decisions

Specific investment decisions use DCF techniques to evaluate different options.

Topic List

Lease or buy

Asset replacement

Capital rationing

Leases where the lessor retains most of the risks of ownership

- Normally short-term
- Lessor responsible for servicing and maintenance

Leases where the lessee retains most of the risks of ownership

- Often long-term
- Lessee responsible for servicing and maintenance

Advantages of leasing

- ✓ Supplier paid in full
- ✓ Lessor receives (taxable) income and tax depreciation
- ✓ Help lessee's cash flow
- ✓ Cheaper than bank loan?

Sale and leaseback

Is when a business agrees to sell one of its assets to a financial institution and leases it back.

Steps in lease or buy decision for tax-paying organisation

1   Calculate the **costs of leasing** (lease payments, lost capital allowances, lost scrap revenue)

2   Calculate the **benefits of leasing** (saved outlay on purchase, tax on lease payments)

3   Discount at the **post-tax cost of debt**

4   Calculate the **NPV** (if positive, lease is cheaper than post-tax cost of loan)

An **alternative method** is to evaluate the NPV of the cost of the loan and the NPV of the lease separately and choose the cheapest option.

11: Specific investment decisions

Equivalent annual cost method

When an asset is being replaced with an identical asset, the **equivalent annual cost method** can be used to calculate an **optimum replacement cycle**.

1 Calculate present value of costs for each replacement cycle over one cycle only.

2 Turn present value of costs for each replacement cycle into equivalent annual cost:

$$\frac{\text{PV over one replacement cycle}}{\text{Cumulative PV factor for number of years in one cycle}}$$

Capital rationing

Is where a company has a limited amount of money to invest and investments have to be compared in order to allocate monies most effectively.

Soft capital rationing
Internal factors

- Reluctance to surrender control
- Wish only to use retain earnings
- Reluctance to dilute EPS
- Reluctance to pay more interest
- Capital expenditure budgets

Relaxation of capital constraints

- Joint ventures
- Licensing/franchising
- Contracting out
- Other sources of finance

Hard capital rationing
External factors

- Depressed stock market
- Restrictions on bank lending
- Conservative lending policies
- Issue costs

11: Specific investment decisions

Profitability index

$$PI = \frac{\text{PV future cash flows (excluding capital investment)}}{\text{PV capital investment}}$$

Assumptions

- Opportunity to undertake project lost if not taken during capital rationing period
- Compare uncertainty about project outcomes
- Projects are divisible
- Ignore strategic value
- Ignore cash flow patterns
- Ignore project sizes

Example

Project A has investment of $10,000, present value of cash inflows $11,240

Project B has investment of $40,000, present value of cash inflows $43,801

Project B has higher NPV ($3,801 compared with $1,240)

Project A has higher PI (1.12 compared with 1.10)

12: Sources of finance

Topic List

Short-term sources of finance

Debt finance

Venture capital

Equity finance

Islamic finance

This chapter covers a range of sources of short and long-term finance. Section B questions may require a discussion of sources of finance.

Overdrafts v loans

Overdrafts

- Designed for day to day help
- Only pay interest when overdrawn
- Bank has flexibility to review
- Can be renewed
- Won't affect gearing calculation

Loans

- Medium-term purposes
- Interest and repayments set in advance
- Bank won't withdraw at short notice
- Shouldn't exceed asset life
- Can have loan-overdraft mix
- Loan interest rate usually lower than o/d rate

Trade credit

- An interest-free short-term loan
- Risks loss of supplier goodwill
- Cost is loss of early payment discounts

Operating leases

- A contract between the lessor and the lessee for the hire
- Lessor responsible for servicing and maintenance

Debt finance

- Availability depends on size of business
- Duration of required finance
- Fixed or floating rate?
- Security and covenants?

Deep discount bonds

Are issued at a large discount to the nominal value of the bonds.

Zero coupon bonds

Are issued at a discount, with no interest paid on them.

Redemption

Is the repayment of bonds at maturity.

Convertible bonds

Give the holder the right to convert to other securities, normally ordinary shares, at a pre-determined price/rate and time.

Conversion premium = Current market value of bonds − Conversion value of bonds

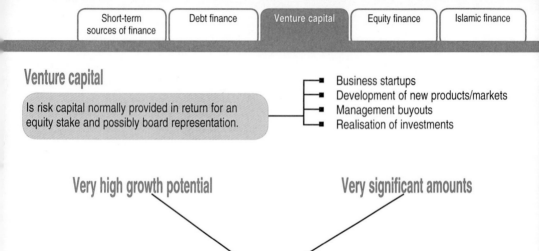

Venture capital

Is risk capital normally provided in return for an equity stake and possibly board representation.

- Business startups
- Development of new products/markets
- Management buyouts
- Realisation of investments

Very high growth potential

Very significant amounts

Very high returns

Equity finance

Is raised through the sale of ordinary shares to investors via a new issue or a rights issue.

Stock market listing

→ Access to wider pool of equity finance
→ Higher public profile
→ Higher investor confidence due to greater scrutiny
→ Allows owners to realise some of their investment
→ Allows use of share issues for incentive schemes and takeovers

Disadvantages of obtaining listing

- [X] Loss of control
- [X] Vulnerability to takeover
- [X] More scrutiny
- [X] Greater restrictions on directors
- [X] Compliance costs

Initial public offer (IPO)

The company sells shares to the public at large for the first time. Offer for sale by tender means allotting shares at the highest price they will be taken up.

Costs of share issues

- Underwriting costs
- Stock Exchange listing fees
- Issuing house, solicitors, auditors or public relations fees
- Printing and distribution costs
- Advertising

Placing

Placing means arranging for most of an issue to be bought by a small number of institutional investors. It is cheaper than an IPO.

Pricing share issues

- Price of similar companies
- Current market conditions
- Future trading prospects
- Premium on launch
- Price growth after launch
- Higher price means fewer shares and less earnings dilution

Rights issue

Is an offer to existing shareholders enabling them to buy new shares.

→ Offer price will be lower than current market price of existing shares.

Advantages of rights issue

☑ Lower issue costs than IPO

☑ Shareholders acquire more shares at discount

☑ Relative voting rights unaffected

Value of rights
Theoretical ex-rights price – Issue price

TERP example

	$
4 shares @ $2.00	8.00
1 share @ $1.50	1.50
5	9.50

$$\text{TERP} = \frac{9.50}{5} = \$1.90$$

Islamic finance transaction	Similar to	Differences
Murabaha	Trade credit/loan	Pre-agreed mark up to be paid, in recognition of convenience of paying later, for an asset transferred now. No interest charged.
Musharaka	Venture capital	Profits shared according to a pre-agreed contract. No dividends paid. Losses shared according to capital contribution.
Mudaraba	Equity	Profits shared according to a pre-agreed contract. No dividends paid. Losses solely attributable to the provider of the capital.
Ijara	Leasing	In ijara the lessor still owns the asset and incurrs the risk of ownership. The lessor is responsible for major maintenance and insurance.
Sukuk	Bonds	There is an underlying tangible asset that the sukuk holder shares in the risk and rewards of ownerships. This gives the sukuk properties of equity finance as well as debt finance.

13: Dividend policy

Dividend policy is an important part of a company's relations with its equity shareholders.

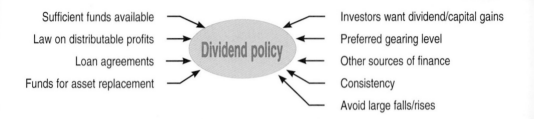

Sufficient funds available → **Dividend policy** ← Investors want dividend/capital gains

Law on distributable profits → ← Preferred gearing level

Loan agreements → ← Other sources of finance

Funds for asset replacement → ← Consistency

← Avoid large falls/rises

Retain earnings

- No payment to finance providers
- Enables directors to invest without asking for approval by finance providers
- Avoids new share issue and change of control and issue costs

Pay dividends

- Signal of good prospects
- Ensures share price stability
- Shareholders want regular income

Young company	Mature company
■ Zero/low dividend ■ High growth/investment needs ■ Wants to minimise debt	■ High, stable dividend ■ Lower growth ■ Able and willing to take on debt

◄──────────────►

Scrip dividend

Is a dividend payment in the form of new shares, not cash.

Scrip issue

Is an issue of new shares to current shareholders, by converting equity reserves.

Share repurchase

Is a use for surplus cash, increases EPS and increases gearing. It may prevent a takeover or enable a quoted company to withdraw from the stock market.

14: The cost of capital

Topic List

The cost of capital

Dividend growth model

CAPM

Cost of debt

WACC

The cost of capital is used as a discount rate in NPV calculations. This chapter looks at how the cost of capital is calculated.

The cost of capital

Is the rate of return that the enterprise must pay to satisfy the providers of funds and it reflects the riskiness of providing funds.

Risk free rate of return +
Premium for business risk +
Premium for financial risk
COST OF CAPITAL

Increasing risk

Creditor hierarchy

1. Creditors with a fixed charge
2. Creditors with a floating charge
3. Unsecured creditors
4. Preference shareholders
5. Ordinary shareholders

Cost of capital if constant dividends paid

$$k_e = \frac{D}{P_0}$$ Exam formula

Where P_0 is price at time 0
        D is dividend
        k_e is cost of equity or preference capital

The growth model

$$k_e = \frac{D_0(1+g)}{P_0} = \frac{D_1}{P_0} + g$$ Exam formula

Where D_0 is dividend at time 0
        D_1 is dividend at time 1
        g is dividend growth rate

Estimating growth rate

Use formula (Gordon's growth model):

$$g = br$$ Exam formula

Where r is accounting return on capital employed
        b is proportion of earnings retained

Or historic growth:

$$g = \sqrt[n]{\frac{\text{dividend in year x}}{\text{dividend in year x} - n}} - 1$$

14: The cost of capital

The Capital Asset Pricing Model (CAPM)

Can be used to calculate the cost of equity and incorporate **risk**.

Beta factor (β)

Measures the systematic risk of a security relative to the market. It is the average fall in the return on a share each time there is a 1% fall in the stockmarket as a whole.

Unsystematic risk

- Specific to the company
- Can be reduced or eliminated by diversification

Systematic risk

- Due to variations in market activity
- Cannot be diversified away

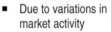

Increasing risk

Beta < 1.0
Share < average risk
K_e < average

Beta = 1.0
Share = average risk
K_e = average

Beta > 1.0
Share > average risk
K_e > average

The CAPM formula

$$E(r_i) = R_f + \beta_i (E(r_m) - R_f)$$ Exam formula

Where $E(r_i)$ is cost of equity capital/expected equity return

R_f is risk-free rate of return

$E(r_m)$ is return from market

β_i is beta factor of security

Market risk premium/equity risk premium

$E(r_m) - R_f$ The extra return required from a share to compensate for its risk compared with average market risk.

Problems with CAPM

Assumptions unrealistic?

- Zero insolvency costs
- Investment market efficient
- Investors hold well-diversified portfolios
- Perfect capital market

Required estimates difficult to make

- Excess return
- Risk-free rate (government securities' rates vary with lending terms)
- β factors difficult to calculate

After tax cost of irredeemable debt capital

$$k_{dnet} = \frac{i(1-T)}{P_0} \quad \text{Formula to learn}$$

Where k_{dnet} is the after-tax cost of the debt capital

i is the annual interest payment

P_0 is the current market price of the debt capital ex-interest

T is the rate of tax

Cost of convertible debt

Use the IRR method as for cost of redeemable debt, but redemption value = conversion value.

$$\text{Conversion value} = P_0(1+g)^n R \quad \text{Formula to learn}$$

Cost of redeemable debt

Year	Cash flow	DF_a	PV_a	DF_b	PV_b
0	Market value	1	(X)	1	(X)
1 – n	Interest less tax	X	X	X	X
n	Redemption value	X	X	X	X

$$K_d = a + \left[\frac{NPV_a}{NPV_a - NPV_b} \right](b-a)$$

P_0 is current ex-dividend ordinary share price

g is the expected annual growth of the ordinary share price

n is the number of years to conversion

R is the number of shares received on conversion

$$\text{WACC} = \left[\frac{V_e}{V_e + V_d}\right] k_e + \left[\frac{V_d}{V_e + V_d}\right] k_d (1 - T)$$

Exam formula

k_e is cost of equity V_e is market value of equity
k_d is cost of debt V_d is market value of debt

Use market values rather than book values unless market values unavailable (unquoted company).

Assumptions of WACC

- Project small relative to company and has same business risk as company
- WACC reflects company's long-term future capital structure and costs
- New investments financed by new funds
- Cost of capital reflects marginal cost

Problems with WACC

- New investments may have different business risk
- New finance may change capital structure and perceived financial risk
- Cost of floating rate capital not easy to calculate

15: Gearing and capital structure

Topic List

Gearing

SMEs

This chapter looks at the effects of sources of finance on the financial position and financial risk of a company. It also considers the particular financing needs and problems of small and medium-sized entities.

Gearing

Is the amount of debt finance a company uses relative to its equity finance.

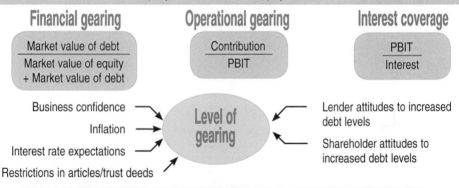

Financial gearing

$$\frac{\text{Market value of debt}}{\text{Market value of equity} + \text{Market value of debt}}$$

Operational gearing

$$\frac{\text{Contribution}}{\text{PBIT}}$$

Interest coverage

$$\frac{\text{PBIT}}{\text{Interest}}$$

Business confidence →

Inflation →

Interest rate expectations →

Restrictions in articles/trust deeds →

Level of gearing

← Lender attitudes to increased debt levels

← Shareholder attitudes to increased debt levels

Gearing increases variability of shareholder earnings and risk of financial failure.

Small and medium-sized enterprises (SMEs)

Have three main characteristics:

1 Unquoted private entities

2 Ownership restricted to a few individuals

3 Not just micro-businesses that exist to employ just owner

Funding gap

High failure rate so hard to raise external finance

Few shareholders so hard to raise internal finance

Maturity gap

Hard to obtain medium term loans due to mismatching of maturity of assets and liabilities.

 Financing problems

Inadequate security

Making banks reluctant to lend.

15: Gearing and capital structure

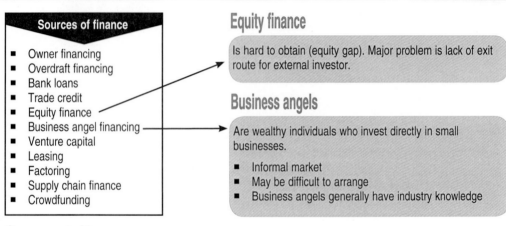

Sources of finance

- Owner financing
- Overdraft financing
- Bank loans
- Trade credit
- Equity finance
- Business angel financing
- Venture capital
- Leasing
- Factoring
- Supply chain finance
- Crowdfunding

Equity finance

Is hard to obtain (equity gap). Major problem is lack of exit route for external investor.

Business angels

Are wealthy individuals who invest directly in small businesses.

- Informal market
- May be difficult to arrange
- Business angels generally have industry knowledge

Government aid

Includes the Enterprise Finance Guarantee, grants and Enterprise Capital Funds.

Supply chain finance

The use of financial instruments, practices and technologies to optimise the management of the working capital and liquidity tied up in supply chain processes, eg selling invoices at a small discount in order to obtain the cash in advance of the invoice due date.

Crowdfunding

The funding of a project by raising money from a large number of people.

16: Capital structure

Capital structure theories look at the impact of a company changing its gearing.

Geared betas can be used to obtain an appropriate required return from projects with differing business and financial risks.

Is there an optimal capital structure?

Traditional theory

There is an **optimal capital mix** at which the weighted average cost of capital is minimised. Shareholders demand increased returns to compensate for greater risk as gearing rises (due to increased financial risk). At high gearing debtholders also require higher returns.

Modigliani and Miller

The weighted average cost of capital is **not influenced by changes in capital structure**. The benefits of issuing debt are counterbalanced by the increased cost of equity.

Pecking order theory

Increasing issue costs

1 Use internal funds if available

2 Use debt

3 Issue new equity

Traditional theory

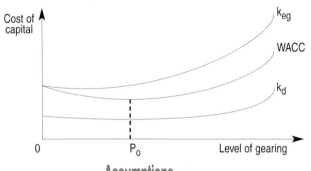

Assumptions

- All earnings paid out as dividends
- Earnings and business risk constant
- No issue costs
- Tax ignored

k_{eg}	is the cost of equity in the geared company
k_d	is the cost of debt
WACC	is the weighted average cost of capital
P_0	is the optimal capital structure where WACC is lowest

M&M – ignoring taxation

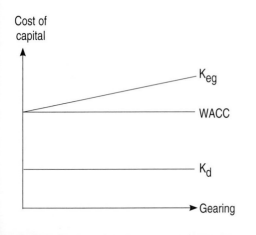

M&M – with corporate taxation

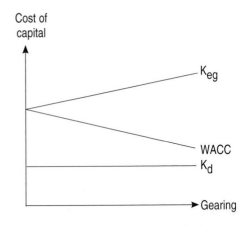

The lower a company's WACC, the higher the NPV of its future cash flows and the higher its market value.

Cost of capital

Calculate using

WACC	**Marginal cost of capital (using CAPM)**
■ Projects must be small relative to company	■ Project has a different business risk
■ Same financial risk from existing capital structure	■ Finance used to fund investment changes capital structure
■ Project has same business risk as company	■ Use adjusted betas

16: Capital structure

Calculating a marginal cost of capital

1. Find a company's beta in the new business area

2. Ungear their beta for their debt, then regear it for your company's debt

3. Use this project-specific geared beta and CAPM to calculate an appropriate cost of capital

$$\beta_a = \left[\frac{V_e}{(V_e + V_d(1-T))} \beta_e \right] + \left[\frac{V_d(1-T)}{V_e + V_d(1-T)} \beta_d \right]$$ Exam formula

β_a = Ungeared (asset) beta V_d = Market value of debt capital

β_e = Geared (equity) beta V_e = Market value of equity

β_d = Beta factor of debt T = Rate of corporate tax

17: Business valuations

Topic List

Asset valuation

Income-based valuation

Cash flow valuation

There are a number of methods of valuing businesses and acquisitions are a key investment decision.

If a business pays too much for a target, it can damage shareholders' wealth.

Range of values

Max ↑	Value the **cashflows** or **earnings** under new ownership
	Value the **dividends** under the existing management
Min ↓	Value the **assets**

Possible bases of valuation

Historic basis
(unlikely to be realistic)

Replacement basis
(asset used on ongoing basis)

Realisable basis
(asset sold/ business broken up)

Uses of net asset valuation method

- As measure of security in a share valuation
- As measure of comparison in scheme of merger
- As floor value in business that is up for sale
- Doesn't value the business as a going concern

Problems in valuation

- Need for professional valuation
- Realisation of assets
- Contingent liabilities
- Market for assets

Price-earnings ratio

$$P/E \text{ ratio} = \frac{\text{Market value}}{\text{EPS}}$$

$$\text{Market value} = \text{EPS} \times P/E \text{ ratio}$$

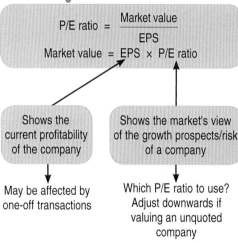

Shows the current profitability of the company

May be affected by one-off transactions

Shows the market's view of the growth prospects/risk of a company

Which P/E ratio to use? Adjust downwards if valuing an unquoted company

Have to decide suitable P/E ratio.

Factors to consider:

- Industry
- Status
- Marketability
- Shareholders
- Asset backing and liquidity
- Nature of assets
- Gearing

Earnings yield valuation model

$$\text{Market value} = \frac{\text{Earnings}}{\text{Earnings yield}}$$

Dividend valuation model

$$P_0 = \frac{D}{k_e}$$

Where P_0 is price at time 0

D is dividend (constant)

k_e is cost of equity

$$P_0 = \frac{D_0(1 + g)}{k_e - g}$$ Exam formula

Where D_0 is dividend in current year

g is dividend growth rate

K_e (or r_e) is the cost of equity

Assumptions

- Dividends from new projects of same risk type as existing operations
- No increase in cost of capital
- Perfect information
- Shareholders have same marginal capital cost
- Ignore tax and issue expenses

Problems

- Companies that don't pay dividends don't have zero values
- Need enough profitable projects to maintain dividends
- Dividend policy likely to change on takeover

Discounted cash flows method

Value investment using expected after-tax cash flows of investment and appropriate cost of capital.

Problems
■ Difficult to select appropriate cost of capital
■ Unreliable estimates of future cash flows
■ Not best method for minority interests who lack influence on cash flows

Irredeemable debt

$$P_0 = \frac{i}{k_d} \text{ or } \frac{i(1-T)}{k_{dnet}} \text{ with taxation}$$

Redeemable debt

$$P_0 = (\text{interest earnings} \times \text{annuity factor}) + (\text{Redemption value} \times \text{Discounted cash flow factor})$$

Convertible debt

$$P_0 = (1 + g)^n R$$

18: Market efficiency

Topic List

Efficient market hypothesis

Valuation of shares

Share prices are determined by the stock market and should provide a reasonably accurate business valuation if the market is at least semi-strong form efficient.

The efficient market hypothesis

Provides a rationale for explaining how share prices react to new information about a company and when any such reaction occurs.

Weak-form efficiency suggests prices already reflect all relevant information about past price movements and their implications.

Semi strong-form efficiency suggests prices are also influenced by publicly available knowledge.

Strong-form efficiency suggests prices are also influenced by inside information.

Features of efficient markets

- Prices reflect all relevant information – **information processing or pricing efficiency**
- Funds are directed towards firms which make the best of use of them – **allocative efficiency**
- Transaction costs insignificant – **operational efficiency**

Implications

- The share price of a company is the best basis for a takeover bid.
- A company should concentrate on maximising NPV of investments.
- There is no point in attempting to mislead the market.

Fundamental analysis

Is based on the theory that share prices can be derived from an analysis of future dividends.

Chartists/technical analysts

Attempt to predict share prices by assuming that past price patterns will be repeated.

Practical considerations

Availability and sources of information

Efficiency in a market relates to how quickly and accurately prices adjust to new information.

Liquidity

Is the ease of dealing in shares. Large companies have better liquidity and greater marketability than small companies.

Practical considerations

Market imperfections and price anomalies

Support the view that irrationality often drives the stock market eg seasonal effects, short-run overreactions.

Market capitalisation

Is the market value of a company's shares multiplied by the number of issued shares. The return from investing in smaller companies is greater in the long run.

Behavioural finance

Attempts to explain the market implications of the psychological factors behind investor decisions and suggests that irrational investor behaviour may cause overreactions in prices.

19: Foreign currency risk

Topic List

Foreign currency risk

Causes of exchange rate fluctuations

Foreign currency risk management

Derivatives

You need to be able to explain the risks associated with exchange rate movements and suggest and calculate appropriate hedging methods.

Spot rate

Is the exchange rate currently offered on a particular currency.

Forward rate

Is an exchange rate set for currencies to be exchanged at a specified **future** date.

Economic risk

Is the risk that the present value of a company's **future cash flows** might be reduced by adverse exchange rate movements.

Transaction risk

Is the risk of **adverse exchange rate movements** between the date the price is agreed and the date cash is received/paid, arising during normal international trade.

Remember!

| Company | sells | base currency | LOW |
| | buys | base currency | HIGH |

For example, if UK company is buying and selling pounds, selling (offer) price may be 1.45 $/£, buying (bid) price may be 1.47 $/£.

Translation risk

Is the risk that the organisation will make exchange losses when the **accounting results** of its foreign branches or subsidiaries are translated into the home currency.

Influences on exchange rates

- Interest rates
- Inflation rates
- Balance of payments
- Market sentiment/speculation
- Government policy

Purchasing power parity

Predicts exchange rate fluctuations based on differences in inflation rates in two countries.

$$S_1 = S_0 \times \frac{(1+h_c)}{(1+h_b)}$$ Exam formula

h_c = inflation rate in country c
h_b = inflation rate in country b

Fisher effect

Looks at the relationship between interest rates and expected rates of inflation

[1 + nominal rate] = [1 + real interest rate] [1 + inflation rate]

Interest rate parity

Predicts foreign exchange rate fluctuations based on differences in interest rates in two countries.

$$F_0 = S_0 \times \frac{(1+i_c)}{(1+i_b)}$$ Exam formula

Where F_0 = forward rate
S_0 = current spot rate
i_c = interest rate in country c
i_b = interest rate in country b

19: Foreign currency risk

Four-way equivalence

Links interest rates, inflation, the expected forward rate and the expected spot rate.

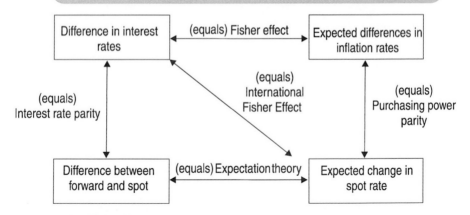

Internal methods include:

Matching

Creating $ costs

Currency of invoice

Invoice foreign customers in their currency

← Revenue in a foreign currency →

Leading

Accelerating receipts/payments

Netting

Against $ costs from other divisions

Lagging

Delaying payments/receipts

Forward exchange contract

- A firm and binding contract between a bank and its customer (an **Over The Counter** contract)
- For the purchase/sale of a specified quantity of a stated foreign currency
- At a rate fixed at the time the contract is made
- For performance at a future time agreed when contract is made

Advantages

- ☑ Simple
- ☑ Available for many currencies
- ☑ Normally available for more than a year ahead

Disadvantages

- ☒ Fixed date agreements
- ☒ Rate quoted may be unattractive

Money market hedging

Future foreign currency payment

1 Borrow now in home currency
2 Convert home currency loan to foreign currency
3 Put foreign currency on deposit
4 When have to make payment
   (a) Make payment from deposit
   (b) Repay home currency borrowing

Future foreign currency receipt

1 Borrow now in foreign currency
2 Convert foreign currency loan to home currency
3 Put home currency on deposit
4 When cash received
   (a) Take cash from deposit
   (b) Repay foreign currency borrowing

Advantages

☑ May be cheaper if an exporter with a cash flow deficit

☑ May be cheaper if an importer with a cash flow surplus

Disadvantages

☒ More time consuming than forward contract and normally no cheaper

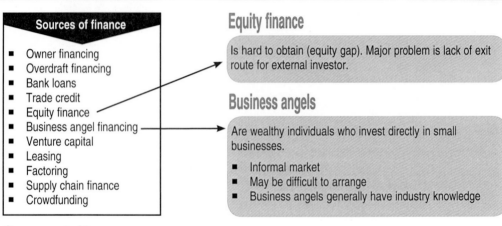

Sources of finance

- Owner financing
- Overdraft financing
- Bank loans
- Trade credit
- Equity finance
- Business angel financing
- Venture capital
- Leasing
- Factoring
- Supply chain finance
- Crowdfunding

Equity finance

Is hard to obtain (equity gap). Major problem is lack of exit route for external investor.

Business angels

Are wealthy individuals who invest directly in small businesses.

- Informal market
- May be difficult to arrange
- Business angels generally have industry knowledge

Government aid

Includes the Enterprise Finance Guarantee, grants and Enterprise Capital Funds.

Notes

Is there an optimal capital structure?

Traditional theory

There is an **optimal capital mix** at which the weighted average cost of capital is minimised. Shareholders demand increased returns to compensate for greater risk as gearing rises (due to increased financial risk). At high gearing debtholders also require higher returns.

Modigliani and Miller

The weighted average cost of capital is **not influenced by changes in capital structure**. The benefits of issuing debt are counterbalanced by the increased cost of equity.

Pecking order theory

Increasing issue costs

1 Use internal funds if available

2 Use debt

3 Issue new equity

M&M – ignoring taxation

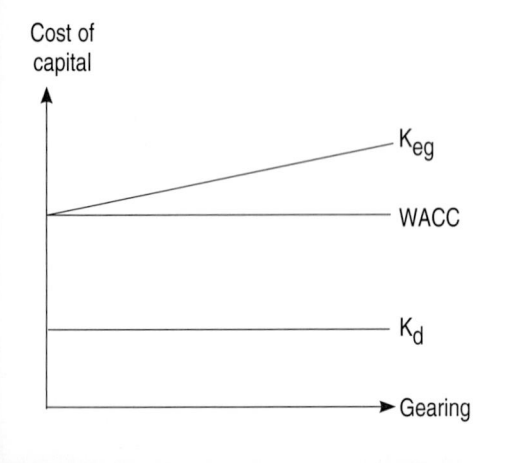

M&M – with corporate taxation

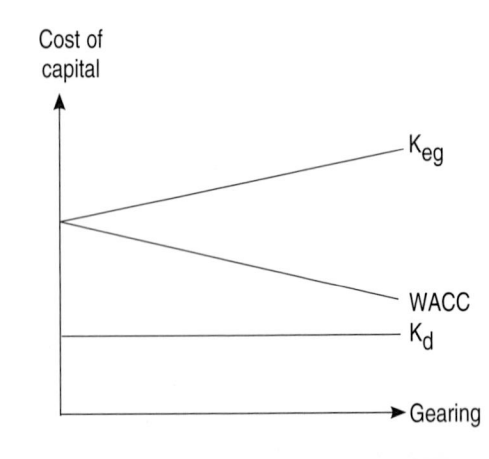

Calculating a marginal cost of capital

1 Find a company's beta in the new business area

2 Ungear their beta for their debt, then regear it for your company's debt

3 Use this project-specific geared beta and CAPM to calculate an appropriate cost of capital

$$\beta_a = \left[\frac{V_e}{(V_e + V_d(1-T))} \beta_e \right] + \left[\frac{V_d(1-T)}{V_e + V_d(1-T)} \beta_d \right]$$ Exam formula

β_a = Ungeared (asset) beta

β_e = Geared (equity) beta

β_d = Beta factor of debt

V_d = Market value of debt capital

V_e = Market value of equity

T = Rate of corporate tax

Range of values

Max ↑	Value the **cashflows** or **earnings** under new ownership
	Value the **dividends** under the existing management
Min ↓	Value the **assets**

Possible bases of valuation

Historic basis
(unlikely to be realistic)

Replacement basis
(asset used on ongoing basis)

Realisable basis
(asset sold/ business broken up)

Uses of net asset valuation method

- As measure of security in a share valuation
- As measure of comparison in scheme of merger
- As floor value in business that is up for sale
- Doesn't value the business as a going concern

Problems in valuation

- Need for professional valuation
- Realisation of assets
- Contingent liabilities
- Market for assets

Dividend valuation model

$$P_0 = \frac{D}{k_e}$$

Where P_0 is price at time 0

D is dividend (constant)

k_e is cost of equity

$$P_0 = \frac{D_0(1 + g)}{k_e - g}$$ Exam formula

Where D_0 is dividend in current year

g is dividend growth rate

K_e (or r_e) is the cost of equity

Assumptions

- Dividends from new projects of same risk type as existing operations
- No increase in cost of capital
- Perfect information
- Shareholders have same marginal capital cost
- Ignore tax and issue expenses

Problems

- Companies that don't pay dividends don't have zero values
- Need enough profitable projects to maintain dividends
- Dividend policy likely to change on takeover

Currency futures

Are standardised (exchange traded) contracts for the sale or purchase at a set future date of a set quantity of currency.

Advantages of futures
✓ Flexible dates ie a September futures contract can be used on any day up to the end of September.

Disadvantages of futures
✗ Only available in large contract sizes
✗ Deposit needs to be topped up on a daily basis if the contract is incurring losses

Currency options

Are the right to buy (call) or sell (put) a foreign currency at a specific exchange rate at a future date.

Advantages of options
✓ Flexible dates (like a future)
✓ Allow a company to take advantage of favourable movements in exchange rates. **Options are the only form of hedging that does this**
✓ Useful for uncertain transactions, can be sold if needed

Disadvantages of options
✗ Only available in large contract sizes
✗ Expensive

Currency futures

Are standardised (exchange traded) contracts for the sale or purchase at a set future date of a set quantity of currency.

Advantages of futures	Disadvantages of futures
☑ Flexible dates ie a September futures contract can be used on any day up to the end of September.	☒ Only available in large contract sizes ☒ Deposit needs to be topped up on a daily basis if the contract is incurring losses

Currency options

Are the right to buy (call) or sell (put) a foreign currency at a specific exchange rate at a future date.

Advantages of options	Disadvantages of options
☑ Flexible dates (like a future) ☑ Allow a company to take advantage of favourable movements in exchange rates. **Options are the only form of hedging that does this** ☑ Useful for uncertain transactions, can be sold if needed	☒ Only available in large contract sizes ☒ Expensive

20: Interest rate risk

Interest rate fluctuations are a source of risk for a business and can be managed using financial instruments.

Types of interest rate risk

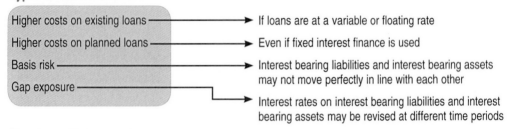

Higher costs on existing loans ——————→ If loans are at a variable or floating rate

Higher costs on planned loans ——————→ Even if fixed interest finance is used

Basis risk ——————→ Interest bearing liabilities and interest bearing assets may not move perfectly in line with each other

Gap exposure ——————→ Interest rates on interest bearing liabilities and interest bearing assets may be revised at different time periods

Structure of interest rates

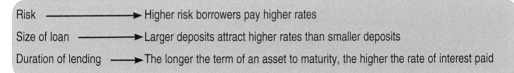

Risk ——————→ Higher risk borrowers pay higher rates

Size of loan ——————→ Larger deposits attract higher rates than smaller deposits

Duration of lending ——————→ The longer the term of an asset to maturity, the higher the rate of interest paid

Yield curve

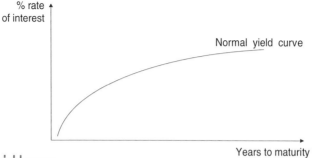

% rate of interest

Normal yield curve

Years to maturity

Explanation of yield curve

Expectations theory ⟶ Interest rates are expected to rise in the future (if expected to fall, yield curve is less steep or downward sloping)

Liquidity preference theory ⟶ Investors require compensation for sacrificing liquidity on long-dated bonds, hence generally upward sloping

Market segmentation theory ⟶ Banks prefer short-dated bonds and pension funds prefer long-dated bonds ie, there are different markets and investors will not switch segment even if forecast of future interest rates changes, hence often kinked or discontinuous

Internal methods

Matching

Is where assets and liabilities with a common interest rate are matched. Used by banks.

Smoothing

Is where a company keeps a balance between its fixed rate and floating rate borrowing.

External methods

1 Forward rate agreements

Hedge interest rate risk by fixing the rate on the future borrowing.

2 Interest rate futures

Hedge against interest rate movements. The terms, amounts and periods are standardised.

- The futures prices will vary with changes in interest rates.
- Outlay to buy futures is less than buying the financial instrument.

3 Interest rate swaps

Are agreements where parties exchange interest rate commitments.

4 Interest rate option

Grants the buyer the right to deal at an agreed interest rate at a future maturity date.

- If a company needs to hedge **borrowing, purchase put options.**
- If a company needs to hedge **lending, purchase call options.**
- **Interest rate cap** sets an interest rate ceiling.
- **Interest rate floor** sets lower limit to interest rates.

Which instruments to use?

Consider:

- Cost
- Flexibility
- Expectations
- Ability to benefit from favourable interest rate movements

Q6. Sensitivity of project to Sales.

Ans 135   105775 $\frac{5775}{105775} \times 100 =$

Q8. Real Cost of Capital?

Ans 114

Q9. Accounting rate of Return.

Ans 145

10. Which discount Rate?.

Ans. 128

$$Avg = \frac{255000}{450000}$$

Cross check

Question 11

Q6.
Q9.
Q11
Q14.
~~Q17~~
Q24.